The Emotional Acts:
Have You Forgotten Logic?
Volume 1

TABLE OF CONTENT

Introduction to Emotions and Logic III
CHAPTER ONE 1
   Historical perspectives on the relationship between emotions and logic 1
CHAPTER TWO 6
   The Power of Emotional Intelligence 6
CHAPTER THREE 13
   The Rational Mind: Embracing Logic 13
CHAPTER FOUR 20
   The Psychology Of Emotions 20
CHAPTER FIVE 27
   Emotional Decision Making 27
CHAPTER SIX 35
   Cognitive Biases and Emotional Distortions 35
CHAPTER SEVEN 43
   Emotional Regulation Techniques 43
CHAPTER EIGHT 47
   The Art Of Empathy 47
CHAPTER NINE 52
   Mindfulness And Emotional Awareness 52
CHAPTER TEN 57
   Cultivating Emotional Balance 57
CHAPTER ELEVEN 63
   OVERCOMING EMOTIONAL CHALLENGES 63
CHAPTER TWELVE 70
   EMOTONAL WELLNESS AND SELF-CARE 70
CHAPTER THIRTEEN 76
   Communication And Emotional Expression 76
CHAPTER FOURTEEN 83
   The Journey Of Emotional Mastery 83
CHAPTER FIFTEEN 91
   Integrating Emotions And Logic 91

Disclaimer

This book offers insights and perspectives on emotions and life experiences. The author is not a certified mental health professional, and the content is not intended as professional advice or treatment. Readers are encouraged to seek professional guidance for individual mental health needs. The book aims to inspire reflection and personal growth through alternative viewpoints on emotions.

By reading this book, you acknowledge that the content is not a substitute for professional advice. The author and publisher do not assume liability for any consequences resulting from the use of the book's content.

Introduction to Emotions and Logic

The human mind is an evolutionary marvel that within it accommodates two apparently antagonistic forces: the stormy sea of emotions and the beaded lighthouse of logic. For a long time, these two elements of our mental landscape have been portrayed as enemies wrestling for mastery over our thoughts and actions. But what if this contrast is more myth than fact?

Imagine feelings and logic not as opposite ends of some sort but as two instruments in the grand symphony that human cognition is. Emotions provide the melody the raw, visceral essence of experience through their answering blips and intuitive flashes. Logic provides the underlying structure: the rhythm and harmony that give shape to our thoughts and decisions.

This interplay between emotion and reason, however, is not a modern discovery; it is as old a dance as man is. From gut feelings that kept our cave ancestors alive in a hostile world to complex algorithms of artificial intelligence, which try to replicate something so human like as decision making the story of emotions and logic goes on to intrigue and challenge us.

As we embark on this journey, we are going to unwind the historical threads that underpin our understanding of emotions and logic. We'll examine the evolutionary crucible in which our emotional responses were forged and observe how these ancient adaptations fare in our modern world. We will view the subtle ways through which emotions and logic interact in some remarkable psychological studies, which give us insights often running contrary to what we might think, uncovering surprising truths about human nature.

This will be a journey that will challenge some of our presuppositions about the place of emotions in what we consider to be rational thought and the rational underpinning of our emotional lives. It's a voyage that will redefine our understanding of choice, morality and the very essence of what it means to be human.

Thus, let us dismiss ideas about emotion versus reason and embrace a more sophisticated view instead one in which reason and feeling prove not to be opponents but rather collaborators in the complex tapestry of human cognition.

CHAPTER ONE

Historical perspectives on the relationship between emotions and logic

The interplay between emotions and logic has been scrutinized by philosophers and scientists for thousands of years. Ancient Greek philosophers, most notably Plato and Aristotle, wrestled with what role the emotions played in human reasoning. Plato believed that the emotions were disruptive to rational thought and thus must be rigidly controlled. By contrast, Aristotle considered emotions integral to human nature and ethics.

Through the Enlightenment, reason came to be apotheosis as the height of human faculties. Philosophers like Descartes focused on the role of rational thought in leading to truth and often classified feelings as stumbling blocks to it. It is during this period that the "reason versus passion" dichotomy begins to impress its mark upon Western thought.

The late 18th to early 19th century Romantic movement dealt a challenge to such a perception about human nature and the expressive psyche, pointing out that emotions account for the greater part of human experience and creativity. Philosophers like David Hume felt that reason alone was not sufficient to bring out morality in judgment and that emotions played a key role in decision making.

The 20th century really changed the character of understanding. Psychoanalytic theory brought out by Freud revealed the unconscious drivers of emotions in human behavior. Much later, cognitive scientists started embracing emotions as intrinsic parts of choice processes, not just a hurdle to clear on the path to rationality.

The distinction between reason and emotion was rendered even fuzzier by recent neuroscience. Research by Antonio Damasio and others has shown that subjects with emotional deficits generally display poor decision making, since emotions appear to be involved in what is considered rational thinking.

❖ **The evolutionary function of the emotions and their connection with survival.**

Emotions evolved to be fast response mechanisms very essential for survival in our ancestral environments. They had and still serve a number of key functions:

- **Fast decision making:** At the point of activation, emotions lead to immediate responses to some events, especially threats. This process bypasses slower cognitive reasoning and may sometimes have meant the difference between life and death in risky situations.
- **Social bonding:** The emotions of love, compassion and guilt provide for social bonding, which is essential to survive in a

group. Such emotions glue family and tribe together and lead to cooperation and mutual help.
- **Motivation:** The feelings of desire and curiosity motivate exploration behavior and, thereby, expose an animal to new resources and learning conditions. In turn, disgust protects from harmful substances or situations.
- **The formation of memories:** Due to this bias, emotionally charged events are better remembered and thus help the organism learn from important experiences and avoid potential dangers in the future.
- **Communication:** Facial expressions and body language associated with emotional states give rise to rapid, non verbal communication in groups, enhancing coordination and warning systems.
- **Enforcement of behavior:** Positive emotions, such as pleasure, serve to reinforce positive behaviors, while negative emotions discourage risky behavior.

These evolutionary adaptations may, therefore, sometimes appear poorly suited in modern environments. For example, a fear response that once helped us avoid predators may now turn up as anxiety in situations that are not threatening. Emotions, however, persist to form a core constituent of our decision making, interpersonal relations and emotional well being.

❖ Famous psychological studies on the interplay between emotions and logic

A number of seminal studies have shed light onto the sophisticated interactions among emotions and logic:

- **The Ultimatum Game (Güth, Schmittberger and Schwarze, 1982)** was an economic experiment that showed that people refuse offers that are unfair to them, even in cases in which it makes no financial sense. It underlined how emotional reactions to injustice may overcome rational self interest.
- **Iowa Gambling Task (Bechara et al., 1994):** This experiment proved that subjects with lesions on their ventromedial prefrontal cortex, which is responsible for emotions, made bad decisions with intact cognitive skills. It therefore drew the inference that the processing of emotions plays a very important role in decision making with advantageous outcomes.
- **Cognitive Dissonance experiment by Festinger and Carlsmith, 1959:** This proved how a person modifies his/her attitudes to belittle the discomfort experienced from holding two contradictory ideas. This focuses on the emotional part of belief formation and its maintenance.
- **Affect heuristic by Slovic et al., 2002:** This study showed that most of the decisions people take are shortcuts, especially

judgments involving risks and benefits by relying on emotional responses.

- **Facial Feedback Hypothesis studies:** Strack, Martin and Stepper tested the theory that facial expressions affect emotional experiences in 1988. They showed that when people experienced certain facial expressions, they then reported feeling that emotion. This proved a two way physiological response with subjective feelings.
- **Somatic Marker Hypothesis by Damasio, 1994:** In essence, this theory was derived from clinical observations and experimental evidence suggesting that emotional processes assist behavior more precisely, decision making by using bodily sensations associated with previous experiences.

These and many other studies have changed our view of the emotion logic relationship. They had established that emotions not only are some kind of disruptive forces but form an integrated part of such apparently rational processes as decision making, moral judgment and social interaction. This research has created an important impact in domains ranging from psychology and neuroscience to economics and artificial intelligence.

CHAPTER TWO

The Power of Emotional Intelligence

While grasping the intricate dance between emotions and logic is essential, there will perhaps be occasions where one needs to bridge this chasm. To this very end, the concept of Emotional Intelligence popularized by Daniel Goleman back in 1995 finds its roots in those very notions of how these two worlds interact. Coined in the 1990s by John Mayer and Peter Salovey, two psychologists, brought to prominence through Daniel Goleman, EI represents the ability to recognize, understand and manage our own emotions and that of others.

Far from being an amorphous skill, emotional intelligence emerged as a critical factor of success both in person and in professional circles, providing the powerful toolkit to sail through the complexities of human interaction and self management.

❖ Strategies for improving emotional self awareness

Emotional self awareness is thus the foundation of emotional intelligence. It refers to the capability for recognizing and understanding our own emotional states, the events that trigger them and their effects on our thoughts and behaviors. This ability must, therefore, be built based on introspection and mindfulness. The ways of enhancing emotional self awareness are:

1. **Emotion Journal:** Record your feelings or emotions frequently to understand patterns and triggers. Note not just what you are feeling but the stimuli for those feelings and what action was taken consequently.
2. **Body Scan Meditation:** This is a Mindfulness technique where there is gradual focusing on parts of the body that allow a person to identify physical manifestations of emotions.
3. **Emotion Vocabulary Expansion:** Expanding your emotional vocabulary provides the ability to identify emotions more accurately. Instead of "happy" or "sad," it would be "contentment," "melancholy," or "exhilaration."
4. **Feedback Seeking:** Seek honest feedback from close friends, family members or professional acquaintances regarding your expressions of emotions. Their perspective could be filled with insights about your expression of emotions and other blind spots.
5. **Cognitive restructuring:** Challenge your thoughts with "What is the evidence?" to distinguish emotion driven thoughts from pure objectivity.
6. **Creative expression:** Painting, music, dance any creative, expressive activity helps in the exploration and expression of those emotions which are hard to put into words.

7. **Mindful use of technology:** Use mood tracking or emotional check in type apps, but be very careful not to rely too heavily on technology for the interpretation of emotions.

By consistently practicing these strategies, you will develop this level of awareness of your emotional landscape, which will provide you with a solid foundation for further developing better self regulation and interpersonal relations.

- ❖ **Techniques for enhancing emotional self-regulation**

Emotional self regulation refers to the extent through which a person can control and modulate their emotional responses. It does not pertain to killing the emotion but rather responding in a way that actions are goal and value serving. Effective techniques on how to improve one's emotional self regulation:

- ◆ STOP Technique: When your feelings begin running high, remember this acronym:

  S: Stop what you're doing.

  T: Take a breath.

  O: Observe thoughts and feelings.

  P: Proceed mindfully.

- ◆ **Cognitive Reappraisal:** A goal to re conceptualize situations and their content to change their emotional meaning. This includes seeing the challenge as an opportunity rather than a threat.

- **Implementation Intentions:** Make if then plans of how one will deal with triggers to emotions. For example, "If in a meeting, I am angry, then I will take three deep breaths before answering."
- **Progressive Muscle Relaxation:** This is a technique wherein tensing and relaxing different muscle groups aid the user in basking in physical and emotional calm.
- **Emotional Distancing:** Observe the emotions arising in you as if you were a scientist studying them. This creates some sort of psychological distance that may lower the emotional intensity.
- **Mindfulness Meditation:** The practice of mindfulness will develop in you the strength to observe the rising emotions without reacting to them instantly.
- **Physiological Regulation:** Engage in activities with a direct physiological impact on the body, such as controlled breathing exercises, cold water exposure or some other rhythmic movement.
- **Values Alignment:** Check back into your personal values for guidance and perspective on how to handle the situation when you're experiencing emotional turmoil.
- **Delayed Gratification Training:** Be sure to delay rewards on purpose so that you work through the "muscle" of delaying and thus develop self regulation.

By applying these practices in your day to day life, you will improve at commanding and controlling emotional reactions that will lead to more thoughtful actions and improved health.

❖ The impact emotional intelligence on personal and professional Success

Developing emotional intelligence has the most profound effects across all walks of life. At a personal level, individuals with high EI very frequently do the following:

1. Healthier Relationships: They communicate more effectively, empathize readily and navigate conflicts with greater ease.

2. Improved Mental Health: Better emotional management is associated with lower rates of anxiety and depression.

3. Enhanced Resilience: They get back faster to the baseline after a setback or change.

4. Greater Life Satisfaction: Such people seem to get more out of life due to their greater understanding of self and others.

At the professional level, the impact of EI is enormous. Of these, examples include the following factors:

I. **Interpersonal Ability and Leadership Effectiveness:** The leaders with high emotional intelligence inspire more and motivate their teams for a positive work environment.

II. **Better Decision Making:** Professionals combine emotional insights with analysis to make more balanced and effective decisions.

III. **Teamwork:** EI improves collaboration by being more attuned to group dynamics and interpersonal nuances.
IV. **Career Growth:** It has been researched and pointed out that EI acts as a very strong predictor of professional success, much more than IQ, in many fields of work, especially the ones that involve high levels of interpersonal interaction.
V. **Conflict Resolution:** Those who are at higher levels of emotional intelligence can better manage workplace conflicts and actually turn them into opportunities for growth, learning and innovation.
VI. **Customer Relations:** It works in client facing jobs toward increased customer satisfaction and retention.
VII. **Stress Management:** Work related stress can be better managed by professionals who have developed EI, which directly reflects in their productivity and job satisfaction.

Emotional intelligence, however, does not stop at the level of individual success, rather, its influence ascertains through to organizational culture and societal well being. With more and more people developing their EI, we foresee more empathetic, efficient and harmonious interaction at all levels of human engagement.

By recognizing the power of emotional intelligence and consciously working to improve it, we open the path to not just personal or professional success but to a more compassionate and emotionally refined world. It refines the faculties of our emotions, strongly combining with the faculties of our logic to derive a holistic, more practical approach toward life's challenges and opportunities.

CHAPTER THREE

The Rational Mind: Embracing Logic

Having navigated the intricate dance between emotions and logic and having plunged deep into the depths of the power of emotional intelligence, come before the foundation of the rational mind: logic. Where emotions present the colors of our mental landscape, logic provides the clean lines and structures that shape our reasoning. This chapter helps us develop logical powers that supplement emotional intelligence to fashion a better rounded and more efficient set of thinking tools.

❖ Tools for developing critical thinking skills

Critical thinking is the motor of reasoning. It is what allows us to base our arguments on sound and clear analysis and evaluation. Some important instruments with which to sharpen your critical thinking skills are:

a) **Socratic Method:** Develop the fine art of the probing question. Upon receiving a claim or an idea, grasp the self firmly and inquire, "Why?", "How do we know this?" or "What are the conclusions?" This is a method named from the ancient Greek philosopher Socrates, which is very helpful in unearthing assumptions and appraising the cogency of arguments.

b) **Argument Mapping:** This involves the drawing of diagrams that depict the structure of arguments. This would thus involve identification of premises and conclusions and even demarcate their relationship to various parts that make up an argument. Tools like Rationale or Mind-Mup exist for building this maps.

c) **SEEI Method:** When elaborating on ideas, use this framework:
   i. State it
   ii. Elaborate
   iii. give Examples
   iv. Illustrate with analogies or metaphors

This will ensure good understanding and communication of complex ideas.

d) **Bayesian Thinking:** A probabilistic mindset means that instead of thinking in extremes, consider degrees of certainty and update your beliefs with new evidence. It does so by Bayes' theorem and provides a better approach to managing uncertainty.

e) **Counterfactual Reasoning:** Develop a habit of envisioning alternative scenarios. "What if things were different?" This tool takes creativity higher in problem solving and helps identify causal relationships.

f) **Concept triangulation:** As you research a new concept, try to find various perspectives from different sources. This works to save you from getting stuck at a small level of understanding and helps build resilience into getting to a more extensive and sophisticated understanding without being victim of single source bias.

g) **Steel Man:** Try to make the best form of an argument the best it can be, rather than attacking the weakest form of the opposing argument, which is called the strawman. This should not only lead to a better formation of understanding but also to more constructive, meaningful debates that can be held with everyone both with partial disagreements.

And, consistently using these, your sharper, more perceptive mind will develop. It will be one that can travel complex intellectual landscapes with sure footed confidence and clarity.

❖ **Logical Fallacies to watch Out for in decision making**

Even the most logical of minds are not immune from logical fallacies, which are flawed patterns of reasoning that could lead any of us off course. Bringing these pitfalls into conscious awareness is therefore important for better decision making. The following are some common logical fallacies to watch out for:

a. **Ad Hominem:** Attacking the arguer instead of the argument. After all, a false idea is false, no matter who is speaking it.

b. **False Dilemma:** Offering only two possible options. Often a situation is just part of a long chain of events or presents several options for a convoluted resolution.

c. **Argumentum ad Naturam:** The belief that what is "natural" must be good or right. But this ignores the fact that many natural things are harmful and many artificial things are beneficial.
d. **Slippery Slope:** An argument that the first step will lead through many intermediate steps to a final, undesirable event. But this ignores intervening causes.
e. **Post Hoc Ergo Propter Hoc:** Assuming that since one event followed another, the first event caused the second. Just because two things are correlated, doesn't mean one caused the other.
f. **Confirmation Bias:** Going out of one's way to find information that will confirm one's own views and ignoring information that goes against it. Mitigate this by actively looking for divergent perspectives.
g. **Sunk Cost Fallacy:** You keep your behavior or an activity due to previously invested resources, even when that seems to have become irrelevant. Learn to look at the situation based on the prospects ahead, not back at the investment that already went.
h. **Bandwagon Effect:** You believe it because many other people do. Remember, popularity doesn't prove truth or efficiency.

i. **False Equivalence:** Treating two things as equivalent when they are not. Very often, this includes minor misdeeds with a major offense.
j. **Gambler's Fallacy:** Assuming that what's happened in the past will have some effect on an intrinsically random process. Of course, in genuinely random processes, that isn't so.

Understanding these and many of the other logical fallacies, you will become much better equipped to spot problems with your own reasoning and with the arguments of other people and thus have stronger and more trustworthy ways to reach your decisions.

❖ **Practical exercises to strengthen logical reasoning abilities**

Reasoning logically is like building a muscle. It requires continuous exercise and practice. Following are a number of fun exercises to build this muscle:

1. **Logic Puzzles:** Learn from the masters: play classic logic problems such as Sudoku, cryptograms and lateral thinking puzzles. These kind of games force logical deduction and disciplined thinking upon you.
2. **Debate Club:** Join or start a debate club. Preparing arguments for both sides of an issue hones your ability to construct and deconstruct logical arguments.
3. **Programming:** Teach yourself to code in a programming language. The process of coding involves very precise logical

thinking and trains your mind to automatically use a structured approach to problem solving.

4. **Chess or Go:** Games of strategy—these are games that require making decisions that are based on very long term planning and an overall logical approach. You also learn to anticipate the consequences of actions.
5. **Formal Logic:** To the maximum possible extent, try to solve syllogisms and other kinds of problems based on formal logic standing on your tail. This will help your mind adapt to following the logical structures strictly.
6. **The Scientific Method:** Formulate and carry out simple experiments in everyday life, adhere to the requirements of the scientific method and learn to think empirically and to test your hypotheses.
7. **Reverse Engineer:** Dissect gadgets or systems to understand how they work. Improves capability of rational thinking and comprehension of causative relationships.
8. **Thought Experiments:** Engage in such philosophical thought experiments as the Trolley Problem or the Veil of Ignorance. Basically, these impose on you to apply logical reasoning in moral dilemmas.
9. **Logical Fallacy Hunt:** Analyze news articles, advertisements or political speeches to identify logical fallacies. This sharpens your critical analysis skills.

10. **Predictive Journaling:** Make predictions about future events and record your reasoning. Review these later to refine your predictive and analytical skills.

Featuring these exercises in your daily routine, you are going to gradually enhance your line of reasoning and complement emotional intelligence with strong analytics. This balance will nurture emotional and logical aspects of cognition within you, which will help you in confidently and effectively relating to complexities of life today.

The key is not to become a cold, purely logical entity but to develop the harmonious blending of emotional awareness with logical acumen. So, in this integration, one becomes capable of decisions that are rational and emotionally intelligent, leading to more fulfilling personal relationships and more impactful professional outcomes.

CHAPTER FOUR

The Psychology Of Emotions

❖ Theories of emotion from different psychological perspectives

The study of emotions has been a central focus in psychology, with various perspectives offering unique insights into their nature and function. Let's explore some of the most influential theories:

1. **James Lange Theory:** Proposed independently by William James and Carl Lange in the 1880s, this theory posits that physiological arousal precedes emotional experience. In essence, we don't cry because we're sad; we're sad because we cry. While controversial, this theory highlighted the importance of bodily sensations in emotional experiences.

2. **Cannon Bard Theory:** Challenging the James Lange theory, Walter Cannon and Philip Bard suggested that physiological arousal and emotional experience occur simultaneously. This theory emphasizes the role of the thalamus in emotional processing.

3. **Schachter Singer Two Factor Theory:** This cognitive approach proposes that emotions result from the interaction between physiological arousal and cognitive interpretation. It

suggests that similar physiological states can lead to different emotions based on how we cognitively label the situation.

4. **Cognitive Appraisal Theory:** Developed by psychologists like Richard Lazarus, this theory emphasizes the role of thought in emotional experiences. It suggests that our emotions are determined by how we interpret or "appraise" events, not by the events themselves.

5. **Evolutionary Theories:** Drawing from Darwin's work, these theories view emotions as adaptive mechanisms that evolved to enhance survival. For instance, fear evolved to help us avoid danger, while love promotes bonding and cooperation.

6. **Social Constructionist Theories:** These perspectives argue that emotions are largely shaped by cultural and social factors. They emphasize how emotional experiences and expressions vary across cultures and historical periods.

7. **Polyvagal Theory:** Proposed by Stephen Porges, this theory focuses on the role of the vagus nerve in emotional regulation and social engagement, providing a physiological basis for our emotional responses to safety and danger.

8. **Broaden and Build Theory:** Barbara Fredrick-son's theory suggests that positive emotions broaden our awareness and encourage novel, varied and exploratory thoughts and actions. Over time, this builds personal resources, leading to increased well being.

These diverse theories highlight the complexity of emotions and the multifaceted approaches to understanding them. Each perspective offers valuable insights and modern emotion research often integrates multiple viewpoints for a more comprehensive understanding.

❖ Neurobiological basis of emotions and their connection to behavior

The neurobiological underpinnings of emotions provide a fascinating window into how our brains and bodies work together to create emotional experiences and drive behavior. Recent advances in neuroscience have significantly enhanced our understanding of these processes:

1. **The Amygdala:** Often called the brain's "fear center," the amygdala plays a crucial role in processing emotions, particularly fear and aggression. It's involved in the formation of emotional memories and influences our attention to emotional stimuli.

2. **The Prefrontal Cortex:** This region is vital for emotional regulation, decision making and impulse control. It helps modulate the amygdala's activity, allowing for more nuanced emotional responses.

3. **The Insula:** This structure is involved in interoception our awareness of internal bodily states. It plays a key role in emotional awareness and empathy.

4. **The Hippocampus:** While primarily known for its role in memory formation, the hippocampus also contributes to emotional processing, particularly in contextualizing emotional experiences.
5. **Neurotransmitters:** Chemicals like serotonin, dopamine and norepinephrine play crucial roles in emotional states. For example, low serotonin levels are associated with depression, while dopamine is linked to pleasure and reward.
6. **The HPA Axis:** The hypothalamic pituitary adrenal axis is central to our stress response, regulating the release of cortisol and other stress hormones that influence emotional states and behavior.
7. **Mirror Neurons:** These neurons fire both when we perform an action and when we observe others performing the same action. They're thought to play a role in empathy and emotional contagion.
8. **The Gut Brain Axis:** Emerging research highlights the bidirectional communication between our gut microbiome and our brain, influencing mood and emotional states.

The connection between these neurobiological processes and behavior is profound. For instance, the amygdala's quick processing of potential threats can trigger immediate behavioral responses before conscious awareness. The prefrontal cortex's regulatory function allows for more measured responses in complex social situations. Understanding these connections can inform strategies for emotional regulation and behavior modification.

❖ The influence of culture and upbringing on emotional expression

While emotions are universal human experiences, the way we express and interpret them is significantly shaped by our cultural context and upbringing. This interplay between biology and culture creates a rich tapestry of emotional diversity across the globe:

- **Display Rules:** Different cultures have unwritten rules about when and how to express emotions. For example, in many Asian cultures, there's an emphasis on emotional restraint in public, while some Mediterranean cultures encourage more open emotional expression.
- **Emotional Vocabulary:** Languages vary in their emotional lexicons. The German word "Schadenfreude" (pleasure derived from another's misfortune) and the Portuguese "saudade" (a melancholic longing for an absent something or someone) are examples of emotion concepts not directly translatable in many other languages.
- **Collectivist vs. Individualist Cultures:** In collectivist cultures, emotions that promote group harmony are often valued, while individualist cultures may place more emphasis on emotions that affirm the self.

- **High Context vs. Low Context Communication:** High context cultures often rely more on non verbal cues for emotional communication, while low context cultures tend to be more explicit in their emotional expressions.
- **Gender Norms:** Cultural expectations about gender can significantly influence emotional expression. For instance, some cultures discourage men from expressing vulnerability, while others may have different expectations for women's emotional behavior.
- **Family Dynamics:** Early family experiences shape our emotional patterns. Attachment styles developed in childhood can influence emotional expression and regulation throughout life.
- **Historical and Socioeconomic Factors:** A society's historical experiences and economic conditions can shape collective emotional tendencies. For example, cultures that have experienced significant hardship may develop unique ways of expressing resilience or communal support.
- **Religion and Philosophy:** Different belief systems can profoundly influence attitudes towards emotions. Some philosophies encourage detachment from emotions, while others emphasize certain emotional states as spiritually significant.

- **Education Systems:** The way emotions are addressed (or not addressed) in schools can impact how individuals learn to recognize and manage their feelings.
- **Media and Technology:** In our globalized world, media exposure can influence emotional norms, sometimes leading to a blending of emotional cultures or creating new forms of emotional expression (think emojis in digital communication).

Understanding these cultural and upbringing influences is crucial for developing emotional intelligence in our increasingly interconnected world. It reminds us to approach emotional experiences both our own and others' with curiosity and respect for diverse ways of feeling and expressing.

By exploring the theories, neurobiology and cultural aspects of emotions, we gain a more holistic understanding of our emotional lives. This knowledge not only enhances our self awareness but also fosters greater empathy and more effective communication across cultural boundaries. As we navigate the complex interplay between our emotions and our rational minds, this deeper understanding equips us to lead more balanced, empathetic and fulfilling lives.

CHAPTER FIVE

Emotional Decision Making

❖ **Case studies illustrating the consequences of emotional decision making**

Emotional decision making is something that can bring about triumph but at the same time lead to a pitfall. Lets look at some enlightening examples from real life that would showcase the strength and probably the potential pitfalls of choices driven by emotions. These are as follows:

I. **The "Ultimatum Game" in Action:** In a real world application of the Ultimatum Game, it was seen that in small scale societies, people would often do the otherwise irrational act of refusing an offer that was too low, even if it meant they would lose out on any gain, this goes to show how our emotional sense of fairness can sometimes supplant pure economic logic to our detriment.

II. **The Challenger Disaster :** A partial cause of the 1986 Space Shuttle Challenger explosion was emotional decision making. Engineers had warned that the O rings might not hold but the pressure and optimism of keeping to the launch schedule overrode the advice in the minds of management. This is an example of how judgment can be off in situations of high stakes.

III. **The Emotional Intelligence of Warren Buffett:** Contrary to the image of the cold, calculating investor, Warren Buffett attributes a great deal of his success to emotional control. How emotional stability can eventually lead to counter intuitive yet highly successful decisions is well portrayed by his ability to remain calm and even buy more stocks during market panics.

IV. **The "Affect Heuristic" in Healthcare:** A study of physicians' prescribing habits showed that their decisions were often subject to the influence of their emotional reaction to pharmaceutical representatives, apart from being founded on the merits of the drugs. This is an example of subtle emotional influences working in professional judgments.

V. **Iceland's Response to the 2008 Financial Crisis:** Unlike other nations that allowed banks to fail, Iceland did allow banks to fail and prosecuted financial executives. Emotionally, this was satisfying, economically, it might have been risky. Surprisingly, though, it put the country on a course to recovery more quickly than most people had thought possible, sometimes proving that what might seem right emotionally is actually the correct decision.

VI. **The Cuban Missile Crisis:** The handling of the Cuban Missile Crisis is widely regarded as the single master class in the balance between emotion and reason by President Kennedy. He, in all likelihood, staved off a nuclear war by reigning in his first emotional urge to take military action and opted for a naval blockade instead.

These studies show that matters of emotion and decision making are complexly intertwined. They illustrate how emotions may sometimes misguide us, but how they may also provide us with intuitive insights that are useful and valuable. The crux is to recognize emotional influences and to assimilate them with logic in a sensible way.

❖ Strategies for making decisions based on both emotions and logic

Optimal decision making is mostly an effective blend of emotional intelligence and logical reasoning. These are some ways one could try to achieve that balance:

1. **The "Two Column" Technique:** Create two columns on a page, one for emotional responses and the other for logical considerations. Fill both columns out in regard to your decision. This gives you a graphic representation to help you acknowledge the two aspects and work out a meeting ground.
2. **The "Somatic Marker" Awareness:** Attend to the physical reactions in your body to different options. These "gut feelings" can be very informative. Use them as data, not necessarily as a sole driver, of your decisions.

3. **Temporal Distancing:** Project how you are going to feel about this decision in a week, a month or a year. This technique reduces the immediacy of the emotion and helps one look at that situation with a more detached or balanced perspective.
4. **The "Devil's Advocate" Approach:** Deliberately argue against your initial affective reaction. This will reveal flaws in reasoning that might arise through over reliance on emotion and ensure that you think through both sides of the issue.
5. **Emotion Labeling:** Appropriately identify and label emotions related to a decision. It often reduces their power and opens up greater cognitive analysis.
6. **The "SPEAR" Technique:** Pause, Perception of emotion, Appraisal of logic, Expand perspective, Respond. The model guarantees you have paused to make a decision that you believe is legitimate both emotionally and logically.
7. **Find a Dissimilar Group:** Discuss the issue with those who have distinct emotional temperaments and/or diverse styles in solving problems. It's possible that this type of diversity can lead to a more comprehensive viewpoint.
8. **Keep a Decision Journal:** Keep a log of major decisions and try to include both your emotional feelings and the logic behind them. This can be very helpful in recognizing patterns and improving choices over time.

9. **The "Sleep On It" Technique:** Many decisions are not urgently required. Give the unconscious time to do its work. Decisions may be more balanced between emotion and logic.
10. **Scenario Planning:** Think of a few possible results, some emotionally satisfying and some logical in consequence. That would expand your thought process and would emotionally prepare you to face what otherwise would be considered viable options.

If one adopts such methodologies, one can arrive at a logical yet emotionally fulfilling decision and this increases one's confidence and makes one feel stronger when it comes to making a choice.

❖ Steps to take when emotions are running high in decision-making situations

High stakes situations set off strong emotions in us, which may become overwhelming to our logical faculties. This is a step by step take on how to sail through such tough moments:

1. **Identify the Emotional State:** The first and foremost thing to do is to recognize the fact that you are in a highly emotional state. Sometimes, just by realizing it, you are provided a moment of pause, saving you from acting on impulse.
2. **Practice Grounding Techniques:** Use such techniques as deep breathing, the 5 4 3 2 1 exercise or progressive muscle relaxation to tamp down on the physiological reaction. This reduces the intensity of the emotional experience.

3. **Take Physical Distance:** All efforts should be made to physically leave the present situation, if at all possible. Take a walk around the block, change physical location. Sometimes getting away and returning offers perspective and reduces emotional reactivity.
4. **Identify the Emotions**: Specifically identify and name the emotions one is feeling. This activates the prefrontal cortex, bringing regulation to the limbic system's emotional response.
5. **Delay the Decision:** Unless there is an absolute necessity to make an immediate decision, give in to delayed gratification. Define a specific time in which to revisit. Emotions will have dissipated by then.
6. **Seek an Emotional Outlet:** Vent that emotion in a healthy way, such as talking to a good friend, writing about it in a journal or going out for a run. It would clear some of that emotional surge related to your decision.
7. **Do a Cognitive Check:** Ask yourself evidence based questions such as, "What's the evidence in support of my current thoughts?" or "If this were happening to someone else, what would be my perspective on it?" Doing so would put your rational mind into gear.
8. **Refer to a Pre decided Process:** Create a definite process to refer to before high pressure situations. This "emotional

emergency plan" can give a certain order to your actions wherever you are feeling overwhelmed.

9. **Look for Diverse Perspectives:** Discuss with people who are less emotionally attached to the situation. Their more detached viewpoint can help you get some very valuable balance.

10. **Visualization Techniques:** Imagine yourself successfully going through the process calmly and confidently. This can serve to reduce anxiety and enhance your real performance.

11. **Break Down the Decision:** If the total decision seems too difficult, break it up into smaller, more doable parts. Tackle each small segment instead.

12. **Make a Future Self Check:** Imagine what your future self would want you to do about this situation. This can serve to give both emotional comfort and logical guidance.

13. **Apply the "HALT" Check:** Check if you are hungry, angry, lonely or tired. Most of these states affect your decision making physically and emotionally. Satisfy these simpler needs first.

Recall from our discussions that the idea is not to remove emotions from the process but that they might inform, but do not dominate the choices. By following this procedure, you can use the intuitive power of your emotions and still maintain clarity in logical thinking.

In other words, emotional decision making is a very complex but core aspect in our lives. Real case studies could bring us closer to the understanding of impact, balance strategies on the thin edge between emotion and logic while in the process and a plan of action during high intensity situations, which might lead us toward more satisfying and robust decisions. This approach will help not only in ensuring better results but also in our growth through learning to negotiate the rich interplay between our emotional and rational selves.

CHAPTER SIX

Cognitive Biases and Emotional Distortions

❖ Common cognitive biases that affect our judgment

Our brains, brilliant and efficient organs, take many shortcuts to process volumes of information we receive every day. While these shortcuts or heuristics, are, for the most part useful, they sometimes deceive us.

Here are some of the most pervasive cognitive biases that influence our judgment:

1. **Confirmation Bias:** One becomes more likely to take out information that supports initially held beliefs and not regard the evidence that speaks against. The emotional charge of these attachments to some ideas, hence, makes it hard to change one's mind, even with great evidence against.

2. **Availability Heuristic:** We overestimate events that are more easily recalled, normally simply because they are more recent or emotionally vivid. For instance, when we hear about the accident involving an air plane, we may overestimate the risks of flying. Statistically speaking, though, it is one of the safest ways to journey.

3. **Anchoring Effect:** When people rely too heavily on the first piece of information they come across in making decisions.

Thus, first impressions can easily sway us in our decisions pertaining to negotiations, pricing decisions and even the awarding of judicial sentences.

4. **Dunning Kruger Effect:** A cognitive bias wherein a person with limited knowledge or domain specific expertise fails to recognize his lack of ability. At the same time, an expert underestimates his relative competence.

5. **Sunk Cost Fallacy:** The tendency to dole out more time, money or effort into something only because past investments have already been made, even when it no longer makes sense to do so. This bias tends to lead to emotional choices at work and in personal life.

6. **Negativity Bias:** The tendency for negative experiences or information to have a greater impact on our choices and behaviors than positive experiences or information. Doubtless, another survival based bias but can also result in undue pessimism and aversion to risk.

7. **Bandwagon Effect:** The tendency to do or believe something because many other people do. We also know it as herd mentality. This is common in the stock market, in fashion and even in the proliferation of bad information.

8. **Hindsight Bias:** Tendency to believe, after an event has occurred, that it was predictable and people should have foreseen it, when in fact there was little or no objective basis

for predicting it. Can result in excessive confidence in one's ability to forecast future events.

9. **Fundamental attribution error:** This refers to a tendency whereby the acts of others are attributed to their personality or character and our own acts are attributed to the situation. This bias has the potential to cause a significant impact in our interpersonal interactions and judgments about the characteristics of others.

10. **Optimism Bias:** It is people overestimating the occurrence of favorable events and underestimate unfavorable events. While this enhances resilience, it may be what leaves us unprepared for the hurdles which are most likely to come our way.

Knowing about these biases is the first step towards their mitigation in our judgment and decision making.

❖ Techniques for identifying and mitigating cognitive biases

Although it's probably impossible to be completely free of cognitive biases, we can still develop methods to spot them and reduce their influence. Here are some effective techniques:

1. **Metacognition Practice:** Engage regularly in "thinking about thinking." Ask yourself, "Why do I believe this?" or "What evidence might I be ignoring?" Such self reflection can help unseat hidden biases.

2. **Devil's Advocate Approach:** Argue against your own view or decision intentionally. It may expose one to confirmation bias and therefore make the viewpoint more balanced.
3. **Probabilistic Thinking:** Consider probabilities rather than thinking of things in absolutes. This might be useful against the tendency to oversimplify complex situations and establish uncertainty.
4. **Diverse Information Sources:** Sources of information should be sought from a diverse and even contrary pool. This would counteract the echo chamber effect and lessen confirmation bias.
5. **Pre Mortem Analysis:** Envision that your decision has failed and consider what could be the possible causes of this failure. The technique works out the blind spots and helps to rise above optimism bias.
6. **Bias Checklist:** Create a personal checklist of the most common biases that appear and refer to it when coming up with important decisions. It creates a cognitive guardrail.
7. **Peer Review:** Share your reasoning process with others and invite them to criticize it. Often, outside perspectives can catch biases that we ourselves are too close or too blind to see.
8. **Quantitative Analysis:** As much as possible, rely on data and statistical analysis rather than anecdotal evidence or gut

feelings. This is one way to get around the availability heuristic and other emotion driven biases.

9. **Time Buffer:** Introduce a waiting period to all non urgent decisions and then take your decisions. This will help overcome impulsivity and allow more reasoned choices to prevail.

10. **Bias Labeling:** If you realize there is a possible bias, explicitly label it. This kind of conscious labeling can lead to a diminution of its unconscious effects.

Such techniques help us build a more fine tuned and balanced approach toward decision making, one that respects our mental limitations while attaining increased objectivity.

❖ How emotional distortions can lead to irrational thinking and behavior.

Emotions, while crucial for survival and health, sometimes have the capacity to distort reality, thereby creating irrational thoughts and behavior. The knowledge of these emotional distortions will help in bringing a balance between our emotional self and our being as rational human beings. The following are some common cognitive errors and emotions that spawn them:

1. **Catastrophizing:** It consists of the expectation of the worst possible outcome in any circumstance. This cognitive error frequently results in paralyzing anxiety or avoidance of

situations for which risks should be taken or where opportunities should be seized.

2. **Emotional Reasoning:** If we feel something, then it must be true. For instance, inadequacy might very well translate into a really irrational deduction that one is incompetent when substantial evidence is available to the contrary.

3. **Personalization:** Taking things personal or blaming oneself for happenings beyond one's control. It may lead to unnecessary guilt and personal harassment, having repercussions on interpersonal relationships.

4. **Black and White Thinking:** Viewing situations in extreme terms, all or nothing. This emotional distortion may result in unrealistic expectations and harsh self judgment.

5. **Overgeneralization:** Broad conclusions from a single event; for example, one setback and "I'll always fail."

6. **Mind Reading:** Assuming we know what others think, often negative. This can result in miscommunications and petty quarrels.

7. **Emotional Magnification:** When events are blown way out of proportion. For example, a slight setback can be viewed as a massive disaster, hence, greatly distressing.

8. **Should Statements:** When we hold tight to rigid rules concerning our own or others' behaviors. These are expectations upon which frustration, disappointment or anger

may be experienced because the reality doesn't meet our emotional demand.
9. **Labeling:** Assigning global, mostly negative labels about self or others on the basis of particular behaviors. This oversimplification may result in self fulfilling prophecies and spoiled relationships.
10. **Discounting the Positive:** Discounting positive events or characteristic and magnifying on perceived negatives.

Emotion is often paired with cognitive bias in an overwhelming scheme of irrational thought. For example, negative bias may enhance catastrophizing by leading one to overly pessimistic predictions and subsequent anxiety driven behaviors.

Among the techniques counter to these distortions are techniques such as cognitive restructuring, mindfulness practices and reality testing. In particular, Cognitive Behavioral Therapy has been tremendously useful in discovering and confronting such irrational thought patterns.

By knowing how cognitive biases and emotional distortions interplay, we are more capable of setting up a balanced approach toward processing information and making decisions. The more conscious one is as to the intuitive power of emotions and their balance with rational analysis, more intuitive power comes into play.

CHAPTER SEVEN

Emotional Regulation Techniques

❖ Breathing exercises and mindfulness practices for emotional regulation

The power of the breath is underestimated in our fast world. Yet, it is one of the most accessible and efficient tools to regulate emotions. Deep, meaningful breathing engages our parasympathetic nervous system our body's natural relaxation response. This can help very rapidly lower stress, anxiety and feelings of overwhelm.

Try this simple technique: Breathe in four, hold it four, then out four through your mouth. Do that for a few minutes, thinking just about the breath. It's called box breathing. It can help lash the body into the present and quiet the mind.

It's with mindfulness working with non judgmental awareness that breathing exercises really pair really well. It means allowing thoughts and emotions without getting caught by them, to create some space between experiences and what the reaction could be. This gives space to make more thoughtful responses in situations.

Quick mindfulness exercise: Close your eyes and bring attention to your senses what do you hear? Feel? Smell? This really very simple process of tuning into your local environment might disrupt harmful thought processes and bring one back into the present.

Developing a muscle takes time and so does perfecting the art of emotion regulation. These techniques should, therefore, be practiced as regularly as possible. Starting with a few minutes a day and gradually increasing the time when one is more comfortable, one can fit it into his daily routine.

❖ Journaling: as a tool for processing and managing emotions.

An empty page can become your very powerful friend for regulating your emotions. Journaling is a private, non judgmental space to help one understand himself better. This is not perfect grammar or fine eloquent prose; this is honest self expression.

Do stream of consciousness writing when one is really overwhelmed. This is a technique where, for 10 minutes, one writes anything that crosses the mind without any inhibitions, edits and censorship. This helps clear pent up feelings and provides clarity of what is really bothering you. Other structured or prompted types of emotional processing might go well with examples like the following:

"Right now, I'm feeling. because."

"Three things I am grateful for today are."

If I could change one thing about my current situation, it would be."); You can also find out your emotional response patterns over time through journaling.

Looking back on a regular basis at what you have written can bring to your notice reasons or recurring themes to these reactions, which you then work on more effectively. Remember, your journal is for your eyes only. This privacy allows for complete honesty, which is very necessary for authentic emotional study and growth.

- ❖ **Seeking support from friends, family or mental health professionals**

While self regulation strategies are very useful in and of themselves, we are ultimately social beings who most of the time need to reach out and find support from other human beings in order to really thrive emotionally.

Emotional first aid is minutes away when you're in crisis just contact someone you trust, such as a close friend or relative. Many times, just talking about our concerns to someone who will listen allows us to get things in perspective. Choose people who will listen without trying to "fix" things for you and who respect your feelings.

It's also important to know when you need more specialized support. That's what mental health professionals are trained for: to offer you tools and strategies tailored to your needs. They can offer unbiased perspectives and evidence based techniques on managing complex emotions.

Seek professional help if:

* Your emotions are impacting your daily life,
* You're coping in unhealthy ways,
* You're hopeless, despondent and it won't go away.

In fact, to ask for help is a sign of strength, not weakness. This shows self awareness and commitment to well being.

By combining these two personal practices with the support of others, you will have a pretty robust emotional regulation toolkit. That's a balanced approach toward emotional well being, resilience and self understanding.

CHAPTER EIGHT

The Art Of Empathy

❖ **Developing active listening skills to enhance empathy.**

Active listening is the cornerstone of empathy, transforming superficial interactions into profound connections. It's not merely about hearing words; it's about absorbing the entire message verbal and non verbal with genuine interest and without judgment.

- **To practice active listening:**

1. **Give your full attention:** Put away distractions like phones or laptops. Face the speaker and maintain appropriate eye contact.
2. **Use non verbal cues:** Nod, lean in slightly and use facial expressions to show you're engaged.
3. **Avoid interrupting:** Let the speaker finish their thoughts before responding.
4. **Reflect and clarify:** Paraphrase what you've heard to ensure understanding. "So what I'm hearing is..."
5. **Ask open ended questions:** Encourage deeper sharing with questions that can't be answered with a simple yes or no.
6. **Validate emotions:** Acknowledge the speaker's feelings without necessarily agreeing or disagreeing. "I can see why you'd feel that way."

By truly listening, you create a safe space for others to express themselves fully. This deepens your understanding of their experiences and emotions, fostering a stronger empathetic connection. Remember, active listening is a skill that improves with practice. Start by focusing intently during one conversation each day, gradually expanding this practice to more interactions.

❖ Practicing perspective taking to understand others' emotions

Perspective taking is the cognitive aspect of empathy the ability to put yourself in someone else's shoes. It involves imagining the world from another person's point of view, considering their background, experiences and current circumstances.

To enhance your perspective taking skills:

- **Cultivate curiosity:** Approach each person as a complex individual with a unique story. Wonder about their experiences and motivations.
- **Challenge your assumptions:** Recognize that your initial interpretations might be biased or incomplete. Ask yourself, "What might I be missing?"
- **Engage in role play:** Mentally place yourself in various scenarios. How might you feel or react if you were in a different position?

- **Read diverse literature:** Fiction can be a powerful tool for experiencing different perspectives. Choose books by authors from various cultures and backgrounds.
- **Practice "both and" thinking:** In conflicts, try to understand how both parties might have valid feelings or concerns, rather than assuming a "right" and "wrong" side.
- **Use empathetic language:** When discussing others' experiences, use phrases like "I imagine you might be feeling..." to acknowledge the limits of your understanding while showing a willingness to connect.

Perspective taking doesn't mean you always agree with others, but it allows for a more nuanced and compassionate view of the world. It's about recognizing the shared humanity in all of us, despite our differences.

❖ Building compassion and empathy through volunteer work or acts of kindness

While empathy can be developed through introspection and interpersonal skills, there's immense value in putting it into action. Volunteer work and acts of kindness provide tangible opportunities to exercise and expand your capacity for compassion.

Consider these approaches:

I. **Local community service:** Engage with organizations addressing issues like homelessness, food insecurity or environmental conservation. Direct interaction with diverse community members can broaden your empathetic scope.

II. **Skill based volunteering:** Offer your professional skills to non profits. This allows you to see how your expertise can positively impact others' lives.

III. **Micro volunteering:** For those with limited time, look for small, one off opportunities. Even brief interactions can be meaningful.

IV. **Random acts of kindness:** Incorporate small gestures into your daily routine. Pay for a stranger's coffee, leave an encouraging note for a coworker or help a neighbor with a task.

V. **Mentoring:** Guide someone in their personal or professional development. This long term commitment can deepen your understanding of another's journey.

VI. **Support groups:** Participate in or facilitate support groups for various challenges. This can provide insight into shared human struggles.

Through these experiences, you'll likely encounter people from different walks of life, each with their own stories and challenges. This exposure naturally expands your empathetic capacity.

Moreover, the act of giving itself can create a positive feedback loop. As you witness the impact of your actions, you may feel more connected to others and motivated to continue cultivating empathy.

Remember, building empathy is an ongoing process. It requires patience, practice and a willingness to step outside your comfort zone. By combining active listening, perspective taking and compassionate action, you can develop a richer, more empathetic approach to life, enhancing both your relationships and your understanding of the world around you.

CHAPTER NINE

Mindfulness And Emotional Awareness

❖ Body scan meditation for improving emotional awareness

Body scan meditation is a very powerful tool to link this missing link between our physical sensations and emotions. It involves the systematic attention of different parts of the body, starting from the toes and moving upward toward the head, just noticing these sensations without trying to change them.

Here are the steps of a basic body scan exercise:

1. Lie down or sit in a comfortable pose.
2. Close your eyes and take some deep breaths, centering yourself.
3. Begin at your toes, noticing any sensations in the body: warmth, coolness, tingling or perhaps no sensation.
4. Now, slowly move up your attention through your feet, ankles, legs and further upward all the way to the top with about 20 30 seconds on each area.
5. If any tension comes into your awareness, simply witness it don't try to let it go.
6. When you find your mind wandering, gently bring your attention back to the area of your body under scrutiny.

The body scan helps increase emotional awareness in several ways:
* It enhances present moment awareness, reducing rumination about past or future preoccupations.
* It helps answer questions about where emotions are first experienced physically for example, anxiety as chest tightness.
* Regular practice will increase overall bodily awareness, allowing for earlier detection of emotional changes.

It does not judge sensations and feelings.

Begin with short 5 10 minute scans and work up in length as you become more comfortable with the practice. Many find it helpful to use guided body scans initially, available through various mindfulness apps or online resources.

❖ **Noticing and labeling emotions without judgment**

One of the major tenets of emotional intelligence is to be able to observe and name your feelings as they come. It is being an observer of your internal landscape without judgment, allowing the acknowledgment of emotions but not getting caught in their story or trying to change them. This skill can be developed by:

1. Having regular time set aside for checking in with yourself by asking, "What am I feeling right now?"
2. Use an emotion vocabulary that is wide ranging. Instead of just "sad," you might feel disappointed, melancholic or discouraged. This nuance can bring subtle insight into your emotional state.

3. Describe your emotions as if you were looking at them rather than being them. For example, "I'm noticing anger" rather than "I am angry." That slight shift creates space between you and the emotion.
4. Avoid labeling emotions as either "good" or "bad." All emotions serve a purpose and bring very useful information.
5. Notice where in your body you feel the emotion. Does anxiety register as a knot in your stomach? Does joy create a warmth in your chest?
6. Be curious about your emotions. You could be interested in their origin or what they might be trying to tell you without necessarily desiring to act on them.
7. Keep a mood tracker or feelings journal throughout the day. Identify patterns over time.

No intention here is to change or even suppress emotions but gain clarity in an emotional landscape. Through this awareness, more considered responses to situations may occur in time and emotional regulation may be improved.

❖ Incorporating mindfulness into daily activities for emotional balance

While formal practices of meditation are extremely helpful, it is the integration of mindfulness into one's daily activities that provides the most profound effects on emotional balance.

Sometimes referred to as informal mindfulness practice, this is attention given fully to simple and mundane tasks.

Here are some ways to weave mindfulness into your daily life:

- **Eat mindfully:** Pay attention to the color, odors, textures and tastes of the foods you eat. Eat very slowly and feel each bite in your mouth. Take note of how the different foods make one feel and affect the energy levels.
- **Mindful walking:** Be present with the ground under your feet, whether walking in nature or just to your car, with every breath rhythm and sights and sounds around you.
- **Mindful listening:** While people are talking, really listen to them. Not only the content but also the tone of voice, facial expression and body language. Notice also your own reactions to what they are saying, but don't immediately act upon them.
- **Mindful breathing:** Take mini "breathing breaks" throughout your day. For example, take 30 seconds to one minute just focusing on your breath. It helps in the moments of stress or before some big meeting.
- **Mindful technology use:** Before you pick up the phone or open your computer, just pause a second. Take a breath and bring to mind an idea of what you're actually going to do with that technology.

- **Mindful transitions:** Instead of instinctively reaching for a distraction in transition times, use them as opportunities to practice mindfulness.
- **Mindful housework:** Transform tasks into meditation just by full immersion in the sensory experience—the warmth of dishwater, the smell of laundry, the repetitive motion of sweeping.

The trick is to have an open and non judgmental mindset with these activities, as you would with formal meditation. Once you catch your mind wandering, gently bring it back to the present moment and the task at hand.

Application of mindfulness in daily life helps in creating a gap between stimuli and the reacting person, thus keeping one's emotional reactions balanced. This in turn can help to reduce stress, bring focus and give an overall feeling of well being.

Remember, mindfulness is cultivated over time. So be easy on yourself and cheer on the small victories of being present. With regularity, you are most likely to grow in sensitivity to your emotions and more ideally placed to meet life's challenges gracfully and in equanimity.

CHAPTER TEN

Cultivating Emotional Balance

❖ **Finding outlets for emotional such as art, music or writing.**

Emotional expression is an extremely potent means for working through one's feelings, gaining insight and creating emotional balance through creative activities. These venues are safe and help in the exploration and release of deep rooted emotions, which often cannot find expression in words.

◆ **Art:** It provides a non verbal outlet of feelings. Be it painting, drawing, sculpting or putting together a collage, you can project your world inside out onto a piece of paper.

a. **Abstract painting:** express emotions by color and shape without having to face the pressure of representative precision.

b. **Feelings wheel:** Using different colors or textures, represent various feelings.

c. **Art journaling**: Mix visual with written reflections.

Remember, it's expression not art. Think process, not product.

◆ **Music:** Music has a way of provoking and processing emotions that few other mediums can. It can be a stimulant to emotional release and a salve to soothe.

Create playlists of music you associate with particular emotions. Then, use them to either accommodate and validate your current mood or to move toward a target emotional state.

Now, if you are a musician, improvise some music that corresponds to how you are feeling right now. Just let it flow; do not judge any of it. Write song lyrics, a form of emotional poetry, even if you do not put them to music.

As far as non musicians are concerned, there can be great depth in the purely emotional outlet that simply involves mindful music listening.

- ◆ **Writing:** Writing is a well structured way of thinking about and detailing one's feelings. It can bring clarity and perspective to complex emotions.
- Journal daily to trace your emotional patterns over some time.
- Do stream of consciousness writing to get at the subliminal emotions.
- Write letters to people or even different parts of yourself, that you might not necessarily mail to express your feelings.
- Take up poetry as a compact, metaphorical means for capturing an emotional state.

The key with any of these outlets is regularity. Make them a part of your regular routine to really feel the full effects of emotional expression and processing.

❖ Establishing boundaries to protect emotional well being

As aforementioned, boundaries play an important role in maintaining the balance of emotional well being. They mark out the lines of where you end and others begin and protect the energy spent on you in the making and maintenance of healthy relationships.

Kinds of boundaries to consider:

- **Time boundaries:** Setting time for personal space, work and relations. Learning how and when to say no not to overcommit oneself.
- **Emotional space:** Identifying your emotions from others. Not being responsible for others' feelings and their feelings affecting you.
- **Physical:** Maintaining personal space and privacy. Communicating on touch/comfort with one's body.
- **Digital boundaries:** Placing a limit on the use of technology and social media to help protect your mental space
- **Work life boundaries:** Setting clear work hours and personal time, especially when working remotely

Now, the steps for creating and maintaining good boundaries are as follows:

1. **Self reflection:** Think of areas in your life where you feel drained or resentful. More often than not, they are indicative of places where you need to establish boundaries.
2. **Communicate your boundaries clearly:** Be direct and communicate with respect. "I" statements will help convey what you need.
3. **Consistency:** Be consistent in enforcing your boundaries. Over time, they will be learned to be respected.
4. **Flexibility:** Equally, allow for occasional exceptions in such contexts when necessary.
5. **Self compassion:** Setting boundaries may be uncomfortable at the very start. Show some patience with yourself while you develop this ability.

Remember that boundaries are not about trying to control others but about being responsible for your own well being. They are a way of respect toward yourself, leading to healthier, more authentic relationships.

❖ Creating a self care routine that nurtures both emotional and physical health

Emotional and physical health is intrinsic in nature, so a wholesome self care routine addresses them together. The steps below will walk you through establishing a balanced self care practice:

1. **Physical self care:**

* **Regular exercise:** Do what makes you happy, whether it is yoga, running or any dance form.
* **Nutrition:** Key attention to a balanced diet that will feed your body and support your mood.
* **Sleep hygiene:** at a regular time with a calming pre-sleep routine.
* **Regular checkups:** Be pro active regarding your physical health.

2. **Emotional self care:**
* **Mindfulness practices:** Add meditation or deep breathing to your daily routine.
* **Emotional expression:** It implies that one should indulge regularly in creative activities like the ones mentioned above.
* **Social connection:** Develop close relationships which can lift and encourage you.
* **Professional support:** Think about therapy or counseling to keep emotional health ongoing.

3. **Intellectual self care:**
* **Learning:** Keeping your mind active with activities such as reading or courses could be a good idea.
* **Leisure:** Do things that are fun to you, that make you feel successful.

4. **Spiritual self care:**
* **Reflection:** This can be achieved by spending time outdoors or simply by journaling, allowing for introspection.
* **Life purpose:** Do things in service of values or your meaning.

5. **Environmental self care:**

* **Organize your space:** Put yourself into a living environment that is calm and supportive.

* **Digital detox:** The concept is to reset yourself by spending less time on devices regularly.

Designing your routine:

- **Start small:** Begin with 2 or 3 self care activities and build up gradually.
- **Schedule it:** Consider these self care activities as non negotiable appointments with yourself.
- **Diversify:** Include different activities that have targeted different dimensions of well being.
- **Be flexible:** Allow your routine to give way to changes as per your needs, which keep changing.
- **Be compassionate towards the self:** if one day you fail to do it, just get back to the routine; no blaming.

Remember, taking care of oneself is not in itself selfish; rather, it's a preconditioning or a requirement for full presence in life and relationships. You can set up the base for well being and resilience by attending to your emotional and physical health.

CHAPTER ELEVEN

OVERCOMING EMOTIONAL CHALLENGES

❖ **Cognitive behavioral techniques for managing challenging emotions.**

Cognitive behavioral therapy (CBT) offers powerful tools for managing difficult emotions by addressing the interconnection between thoughts, feelings and behaviors. These techniques can help you reframe negative thought patterns and develop healthier emotional responses.

1. **Thought Records:** Keep a log of situations that trigger strong emotions. Include:
- ✓ The situation
- ✓ Your automatic thoughts
- ✓ The emotions and their intensity
- ✓ Evidence supporting and challenging these thoughts
- ✓ A more balanced perspective

This practice helps identify cognitive distortions and creates space for more rational thinking.

2. **Behavioral Activation:** When feeling low, it's tempting to withdraw. Instead:
- ✓ Create a list of enjoyable activities
- ✓ Schedule these activities, even when you don't feel like it

✓ Track your mood before and after

This technique can break the cycle of negative emotions reinforcing inactivity.

3. **Cognitive Restructuring:**
✓ Challenge and reframe negative thoughts
✓ Identify common cognitive distortions (e.g., all or nothing thinking, overgeneralization)
✓ Question the evidence for these thoughts
✓ Generate alternative, more balanced perspectives

4. **Exposure Techniques:** For anxiety related emotions
✓ Create a hierarchy of feared situations
✓ Gradually expose yourself to these situations, starting with the least anxiety provoking
✓ Practice relaxation techniques during exposure

This helps desensitize you to anxiety triggers over time.

5. **Problem Solving:** For emotions stemming from concrete problems
✓ Clearly define the problem.
✓ Brainstorm potential solutions without judgment.
✓ Evaluate pros and cons of each solution.
✓ Choose and implement a solution.
✓ Reflect on the outcome.

Remember, these techniques often require practice to become effective. Consistency is key. You might find it helpful to work with a CBT trained therapist initially to learn how to apply these strategies most effectively in your specific situation.

❖ Acceptance and commitment therapy strategies for coping with discomfort

Acceptance and Commitment Therapy (ACT) offers a different approach to emotional challenges. Instead of trying to eliminate difficult emotions, ACT focuses on accepting them while committing to actions aligned with your values. Here are key ACT strategies:

1. **Cognitive Defusion:** This involves creating distance between yourself and your thoughts Label thoughts:
   - "I'm having the thought that..."
   - Thank your mind for the thought, acknowledging it without engaging
   - Imagine thoughts as leaves floating down a stream

These techniques help you observe thoughts without getting caught up in them.

2. **Acceptance:**
   - Practice allowing emotions to be present without trying to change them.
   - Notice where you feel the emotion in your body.
   - Describe the sensation without judgment (e.g., "tightness," "warmth").

- Imagine making space for the feeling, like a beach ball in water.

3. Present Moment Awareness:
- Grounding yourself in the present can prevent rumination.
- Use your senses: Name 5 things you can see, 4 you can touch, 3 you can hear, 2 you can smell, 1 you can taste.
- Practice mindful breathing, focusing on the physical sensations of each breath

4. Self as Context:
- Recognize that you are more than your thoughts and feelings.
- Use metaphors like "I am the sky and my thoughts/feelings are the weather".
- Practice perspective taking exercises to step outside your immediate experience

5. Values Clarification:
- Identify what truly matters to you.
- Reflect on what you want your life to stand for
- Consider different life domains (relationships, career, personal growth)
- Use guided visualizations of your ideal future

6. Committed Action:
- Set goals aligned with your values and take steps towards them, even when experiencing difficult emotions.
- Break larger goals into small, manageable steps.

- Use SMART criteria (Specific, Measurable, Achievable, Relevant, Time bound)
- Celebrate small victories along the way.

ACT's approach can be particularly helpful for chronic emotional challenges, as it focuses on living a meaningful life alongside difficult emotions rather than waiting for them to disappear before taking action.

❖ Seeking professional help when emotions become overwhelming

While self help strategies are valuable, there are times when professional support becomes crucial. Recognizing when to seek help is an important aspect of emotional self care.

Signs it might be time to consult a mental health professional:

1. Persistent feelings of sadness, anxiety or emptiness.
2. Significant changes in sleep or appetite.
3. Difficulty concentrating or making decisions.
4. Loss of interest in activities you once enjoyed.
5. Feelings of hopelessness or worthlessness.
6. Thoughts of self harm or suicide.
7. Inability to perform daily tasks or maintain relationships.
8. Overwhelming stress or inability to cope with life changes.
9. Unresolved trauma or grief.
10. Substance use interfering with daily life.

Steps to seek professional help:

1. Research different types of mental health professionals (psychiatrists, psychologists, therapists, counselors) to understand which might best suit your needs.

2. Check with your insurance provider about coverage for mental health services.

3. Ask for recommendations from trusted friends, family or your primary care physician.

4. Look for professionals specializing in your specific concerns (e.g., depression, anxiety, trauma).

5. Consider online therapy options if in person sessions are challenging due to location or schedule.

6. Prepare for your first appointment by noting your symptoms, concerns and goals for therapy.

7. Be open to trying different professionals if the first one doesn't feel like a good fit.

Remember, seeking help is a sign of strength, not weakness. Mental health professionals are trained to provide tools and strategies tailored to your unique situation. They can offer an objective perspective and evidence based treatments that can significantly improve your quality of life. In crisis situations, don't hesitate to use emergency services or crisis hotlines. Many countries have dedicated mental health crisis lines that provide immediate support.

By combining self help techniques like CBT and ACT with professional support when needed, you can develop a comprehensive approach to managing challenging emotions. This multi faceted strategy can lead to greater emotional resilience and overall well being, allowing you to navigate life's ups and downs with more confidence and ease.

CHAPTER TWELVE

EMOTONAL WELLNESS AND SELF-CARE

❖ **Practicing self compassion and self forgiveness as part of self care.**

Emotional well being encompasses self compassion and self forgiveness, but these are hardly discussed, practiced or at times, never found in the current conventional self care practices. This basically points to the aspect of extending to oneself the very same courtesy and regard that he would give to a good friend.

There are three key constituents for self compassion:

1. **Self kindness:** Be gentle and understanding with oneself, rather than harshly critical.

2. **Common humanity:** Suffering and personal inadequacy are part of the human experience.

3. **Mindfulness:** Gently observing our negative thoughts and feelings with openness and clarity but without judgment, not trying to suppress or deny them.

- **How to develop self compassion:** Begin by engaging in more positive self talk. Challenge your put down thoughts with kinder ones. Instead of telling yourself, "I'm such a loser," say "I'm really doing the best I can in a tough situation."

- Write a letter to your compassionate self: Think about writing to a friend who is going through what you are right now. What would you say to soothe and reassure him or her? Now turn that concern upon yourself.
- Use compassionate touch: If you are distressed, place your hand on your heart or hug yourself gently. This may activate the parasympathetic nervous system, which generates feelings of calm.
- **Self forgiveness is just as crucial:** Recognize the error or perceived failure, but don't judge it. Take responsibility for your choices, but make a clear distinction between the choice you made and your worth as an individual.
- Learn from the experience: What can this teach you? How can you grow from it? Make amends if necessary, but also "amend" your relationship with yourself. Keep in mind that both self compassion and self forgiveness are practices that take time to develop. Be patient with yourself in forming these habits.

❖ The importance of Setting boundaries to protect emotional energy

Boundaries are necessary for emotional health. This protects our time toward more important values and thus we save energy for the same, holding the potential for better relationships. The majority of people, though, find it hard to set up and maintain boundaries. It is because they fear conflict or feel guilty.

Types of Boundaries to Consider:

1. **Emotional Boundaries:** the ability to separate your feelings from others

2. **Time Boundaries:** telling how much time one would like to dedicate to something, then following through

3. **Physical Boundaries:** personal space and comfort levels of physical touch.

4. **Intellectual boundaries:** Your thoughts and opinions are respected by others.

5. **Material boundaries:** Your possessions or financial resources aren't taken advantage of

How to Set Boundaries:

1. **Self awareness:** Anger, resentment or feeling used are often signs that something is violating your boundaries.

2. **Be clear:** Be clear on your limits. What are you comfortable and uncomfortable with? What's non negotiable?

3. **Communicate:** State your limits clearly and directly using first person "I" statements, e.g.: "I need some alone time after work to find my balance."

4. **Consistency:** Apply your boundaries consistently. Over time, people will come to respect them.

5. **Consequences:** Decide in advance on a response when your boundaries are being disrespected.

6. **Flexibility:** While such consistency is important, there must be space for the occasional exception where appropriate and consensual.

It is necessary to remember that setting boundaries is not selfish; it is self respect that lets you be able to show up further with full commitment to your relationships and responsibilities.

❖ Building a support network of friends, family or support groups

A support system is like an insurance plan for emotional well being. They act as a safety net during hard times and a spice during good times. The ways to develop and maintain a healthy support system are:

1. **Find your current support network:**
   - ✓ Identify trusting persons with whom you feel comfortable to open up.
   - ✓ Consider what types of support you have: emotional, practical and informational.

2. **Develop your social connections by:**
   - ✓ Maintaining continuing contact, not just at times of need.
   - ✓ Being a good listener, showing concern for their lives.
   - ✓ Offer back and forth help, if appropriate.

3. **Develop your supports:**

- ✓ Join clubs and organizations related to your interests.
- ✓ Volunteer for what you care about.
- ✓ Take classes and attend workshops to find others with your interests.
- ✓ Be careful with social media to be in the company of people who value what you do.

3. **Consider a group:**
- ✓ Find groups that meet your needs/ concerned group (e.g., a grief, addiction).
- ✓ There are both online and physical support groups.
- ✓ Always remember groups are there for mutual understanding of your experiences.

4. **Develop diversities in circles of relationships:**
- ✓ Well wish for a mix between the relationships of intimate advisors, high acquaintances, mentors, etc.
- ✓ Different relationships can provide different forms of support.

5. **Be realistic in your expectations:**
- ✓ No one source can satisfy all your needs. Distribute your need for support within the network.
- ✓ Be explicit about what kind of support you want, for example, advice, someone to listen to you, practical help.

6. **Establish boundaries:**
- ✓ As much as support is needed, do not over rely on others.
- ✓ Receive the support, but stay an independent individual.

7. **Appreciation:**
- ✓ Continue to appreciate the support.
- ✓ The smallest of things one can do to show appreciation can mean much.

9. **Professional Help:** If necessary, even therapists or counselors can provide more help. They can provide unbiased viewpoints and specialized skills. Remember, building an alliance takes time and effort. So, put in the work and be patient. As you do, you're creating a resource for your emotional wellness: a community that can celebrate your joys and help shoulder some of your burdens.

In practicing self compassion, setting healthy boundaries and building a strong support network, you would have paved up a substantial base for emotional well being. These practices are important not only for negotiating life's challenges in the best way possible but also for improving quality of life and helping you thrive, not simply survive.

CHAPTER THIRTEEN

Communication And Emotional Expression

❖ **Nonverbal communication cues and their effect on emotional expression**

Emotions are conveyed more by non verbal behavior than by use of words. Understanding these non verbal cues and how to use them can be very effective in both sending and receiving messages of emotions.

Some key non verbal cues include:

1. **Facial Expressions:**
   - Micro expressions: Very short, involuntary movements of the facial muscles revealing the original emotions Observe the seven universal facial expressions: happiness, sadness, anger, fear, surprise, disgust and contempt

2. **Non verbal:**
   - Posture: Open postures are indicative of confidence, openness to communication and receptiveness; closed postures may reflect discomfort or defensiveness.
   - Gestures: Hand movement helps emphasize a point or it shows one is nervous.
   - Proxemics: One's use of personal space can be indicative of comfort levels and cultural norms.

3. Eye contact:
- Duration of eye contact, the intensity can express interest, honesty and dominance.
- Averting gaze may express discomfort, lying or submission. This depends on the situation.

4. Paralanguage:
- Tone of voice, pitch, volume, rate of speaking all add to the emotional message.
- Inflections in voice could altogether alter the meaning of words spoken

5. Touch:
- Show comfort, support or affection where appropriate.
- Be aware of cultural differences and personal space.

6. **Appearance:**
- Clothing, grooming affect interpretation of emotions
- Be aware of what your appearance may be communicating in different situations

For effective nonverbal communication:
- **Self awareness:** Take regular checks on your own non verbal cues. Feedback: Share with close friends or colleagues your nonverbal patterns.
- **Tape yourself:** Record interactions to watch your own nonverbal behaviors

- **Mirror others:** Subtly matching others in positive body language can create great rapport

Note that non verbal cues should be mostly congruent, of the same message with the verbal, for clarity. The incongruence between non verbal and verbal sets off the conditions for miscommunication or distrust almost always.

❖ Assertiveness Training to Communicate Emotions and Needs.

Assertiveness is the act of expressing feelings, needs and opinions in an open and clear manner while showing respect for others' rights. It is one of the most critical qualities that provide support for emotionally intelligent communication, thus helping to build healthy relationships.

Key elements of assertive communication:

1. "I" statements:

* Feelings and needs stated from one's perspective

Example: "I get frustrated when others interrupt during meetings," not "You always interrupt me."

2. Be direct and precise.

• Always state what you want or need.

• Don't beat around the bush; never expect people to guess what you're thinking.

3. Listen actively.

• Let the other person know you consider their point of view.

- Paraphrase their response.

4. Use appropriate body language.
- Eye contact.
- Open posture.

  Speak calmly and clearly

5. Practice saying "no": Turn down any request that clashes with your needs or is contrary to your values. Offer alternatives if possible

6. Express positive feelings: Compliment and show appreciation and Mention what others contribute

7. Apply DESC formula in difficult conversations:

* Describe the situation neutrally
* State your feelings
* State what you want to happen
* State the consequences good or bad

Exercises in training in assertiveness:

1. **Role playing:** Practice the response that is to be asserted in various situations with the help of a friend or therapist.

2. **Visualization:** Rehearse mentally and see oneself handling the situation assertively before going into potentially difficult conversations.

3. **Gradual exposure:** Start low level situations and gradually increase to more difficult ones.

4. **Journaling:** Writing out the assertive replies to previous situations that you cannot express yourself on

Remember, becoming assertive is a process. Be patient with yourself and celebrate small victories as you develop this skill.

❖ Conflict resolution strategies for navigating emotional conversations

While conflict is inevitable in relationships, how we deal with it makes a huge difference in our emotional well being and the health of our relationships. Effective conflict resolution means managing one's emotions while working toward solutions that benefit all.

Some major strategies for handling emotional conversations are:

1. **Timing is everything:**
   • Choose a time that both parties are calm and not busy.
   • If feelings start to run high during the talk, be willing to stop and pick up where you left off at a later time.

2. **"I" statements:**
   • State your feelings without placing blame Example: "I feel hurt when plans are canceled last minute" instead of "You always let me down".

3. **Active listening:**
   • Pay attention to the speaker.
   • Paraphrase to ensure understanding.
   • Ask questions for clarification

4. **Identify the real issue:**

• Look beyond surface disagreements to understand underlying needs or fears.

• Ask yourself and others, "What's really important here?"

5. **Focus on the present:**

• Avoid bringing up past conflicts.

• Stay focused on the current issue and finding a solution

6. **Find common ground:**

• Areas of agreement

• Shared goals or values

7. **Solution brainstorming:**

• Lots of options

• Creativity, openness to compromise

8. **Solution chosen and plan formulated:**

• Mutually agreeable solution

• Steps outlined clearly for implementation

9. **Follow up:**

• Check in after implementing the solution to see that it's working

• Be willing to adjust if need be

- **Emotional management techniques for conflicts:**

• Practice deep breathing or other calming techniques

• Use "time outs" when the feelings are too overwhelming

Employ empathy by trying to see things from the other person's point of view.

- Stay clear of character attacks or generalizations (e.g., "always", "never").
- Acknowledge and validate feelings, even if you can't agree with the reasoning.

Keep in mind that the goal of conflict resolution isn't to "win," but to find a solution that best serves everyone's needs. Actually, conflict resolution done well can strengthen relationships through improvements in trust and communication. Equipped with developed nonverbal communication skills, having learned how to be more assertive and having enhanced one's capability for conflict management, you would grow in your skill at appropriately expressing emotions and having fewer awkward conversations. All these qualities pave the way toward the goals of healthier relationships, decreased stress and emotional well being.

CHAPTER FOURTEEN

The Journey Of Emotional Mastery

❖ **Reflecting on personal growth and emotional development over time**

Reflection is a powerful practice toward recognizing and hastening the process of emotional growth. It allows us with clarity regarding patterns, progress and understanding areas that need further development.

Some major elements of reflection:

1. **Aspect of Emotional Awareness:**

 • How has your ability changed in terms of recognizing and naming your feelings?

 • Are you more sensitive to the slight changes within emotions as compared to your past?

2. **Emotional Regulation:**

 • What are some of the changes in strategies to manage very strong emotions?

 • What type of situations are easier or more difficult to balance emotionally?

3. **Relationship dynamics:**

 • How has your interaction with others changed in regard to emotional relationships?

• Do you understand yourself better now in terms of expressing yourself and setting boundaries?

4. **Self compassion:**

   • Has your inner dialogue become more benevolent over time?

   • What do you do to take care of yourself when you are struggling or when things go wrong?

5. **Emotional triggers:**

   • Do you recognize your repeating emotional triggers?

   • How is your response to them different?

Techniques for reflection include:

- **Keeping a journal:**

   • Making regular entries regarding emotional experiences

   • Occasional reviews for repetitive patterns and growth

- **Timeline:**

   • Mapping important emotional events in life and your response to them

   • Notice how similar situations were handled differently over time

- **Feedback seeking:**

   • Ask trusted friends or mentors about changes they may have witnessed in your emotional responses

- **Meditation and mindfulness:**

   • Take time to settle into a quiet state of mind

- Pay attention to your emotions and how they may be approached differently

- **Therapy or coaching:**
  - Professional guidance may provide meaningful insight into your emotional journey

- **Contrasting then and now situations:**
  - Consider how you handled a given type of situation in the past
  - Compare this with what you would do in that situation now, highlighting any differences.

Note that development doesn't always take place on a clean continuum; consider the setbacks as part of the journey, but be attuned to the general trend rather than one off incidents.

❖ Cultivating resilience in the face of challenges and setbacks

Resilience can be defined as the ability to adapt to and recover from adversity. It is an important competence of emotional mastery, whereby one learns how to take life's inevitable setbacks and shocks in stride and in style.

Components of resilience:

1. **Emotional flexibility:**

* The ability to experience a range of emotions without feeling overwhelmed by them
* Skill in shifting emotional states when necessary

2. **Optimistic realism:**

* Hope in the presence of adversity.

* Possibility for growth within challenges.

3. **Strong social support:**

* Nurturing relations that give emotional support

* Knowledge of when, from whom and how to seek help

4. **Problem solving skills:**

* Breaking down big problems into small, workable steps

* Creative thinking about solutions

5. **Self efficacy:**

* Self-efficacy about abilities to cope with challenges

* Confidence arising from successful prior experiences in overcoming challenges

Strategies to increase resilience:

1. **Cognitive reframing:**

- Challenging negative thoughts,

- finding new ways of thinking about events.

2. **Growth mindset:**

- View of challenges as learning experiences

- Adopt the attitude of "yet" for example, saying "I haven't mastered this yet."

3. **Build physical strength:**

- Sleep enough, eat healthily, exercise regularly

- Meditate/deep breathing to destress

4. **Set goals and work for them:**

- Resilience derives from purpose
- Small victories along the way give meaning while moving toward big goals

5. **Learn from adversity:**
   - Analyze what went wrong without self blame
   - Identify lessons for future situations

6. **Cultivate gratitude:**
   - Regularly acknowledge positive aspects of life
   - Find silver linings in difficult situations

7. **Develop emotional vocabulary:**
   - Expand your ability to name and describe emotions
   - This precision can help in processing and managing feelings

Development of resilience is a continuous process. Each challenge one faces is an opportunity to further develop this competence.

❖ Setting goals for continued emotional growth and mastery.

The key to continued growth and overcoming stagnation in emotional development is to set intentional emotional growth oriented goals. It makes emotional mastery active and perpetual.

How to set effective emotional goals:

1. **Self evaluation:**
   - Take inventory of current emotional strengths and weaknesses
     Seek input from trusted others

2. **Visioning:**

• Imagine the type of emotional life you would like to lead and relationship

• What would emotional mastery look like in your life?

3. **SMART goal setting:**

   • Specific: Describe what exactly you want to achieve

   • Measurable: How will you measure success?

   • Achievable: Is it realistic for where you are now?

   • Relevant: Is this something that will help you realize your overall life goals?

   • Time bound: Give it a time frame, which means when should it be completed.

4. **Creating an action plan:**

   • Divide the larger goals into smaller, easily realizable steps.

   • Decide on resources/skills required in each steps

5. **Monitoring the progress:**

   • Periodic reviews of how far down the road you are.

   • Revise either the goal or your strategy where necessary.

6. Recognize and celebrate, even if it is minor; reflect on what was learned along the way.

Example Goals of Emotional Growth:

1. **Better Emotional Regulation:**

* Practice meditation daily for mindfulness for 10 minutes.

* Learn three new stress management techniques and practice during the next month.

2. **Improved Empathy:**
   * Engage in active listening in at least one daily conversation
   * Read at least one emotional intelligence book per quarter

3. **Be assertive:**
   * NEEDS/Boundaries to be expressed in at least one situation per week.
   * Attend an assertiveness training course within six months.

4. **Cultivate self compassion:**
   * Write three self compassionate statements every day.
   * Reduce negative self talk by 50% in three months.

5. **Increase emotional vocabulary:**
   * Learn one new emotion word and use it daily.
   * Keep a journal of emotions in as much detail as possible three times a week.

6. **Improve conflict resolution skills:**
   * Use "I" statements in every argument.
   * Successfully implement a conflict resolution model during the next significant conflict.

Remember, emotional growth is a journey, not a destination. Have patience with yourself and at times when you experience setbacks, look at them as learning lessons. Reassess and adjust your goals regularly to make sure they are still challenging yet within reach.

You will be able to build a framework for continuous emotional growth and self mastery by reflecting on your emotional journey, building resilience and setting intentional goals. Such active emotional development can enable you to foster deeper relationships, improve well-being and basically live up to the meaning of life.

CHAPTER FIFTEEN

Integrating Emotions And Logic

Building on what we learned about cognitive biases, emotional distortions, and the intricate dance between emotions and logic, let us dive into the art of integrating these seemingly opposite forces. The last part will equip you with some quite practical strategies to make holistic decisions but equally emphasize the need for self-reflection and acknowledge the richness of human emotion in our cognitive processes.

❖ **Strategies for making holistic decision that consider both Emotion and Logic**

Emotions and logic do not always have to balance out perfectly, it is the synergy of using their strengths. Some strategies for making decisions that can help one to honor both his or her emotional intelligence and rational faculties are as follows:

1. **The Emotional-Logical Decision Matrix:** Draw a 2x2 matrix with Emotions and Logic axes, plot the choices, and consider how well each one satisfies both your emotional desires and the needs of your logical consideration. Seeing this in black and white should give clarity needed to make decisions that satisfy both criteria.

2. **The "Three Selves" Technique:** Consult your past, present and future selves in reaching a decision. Your past self provides the

emotional context and learned experiences; your present self, the immediate emotional and logistic input and your future self, long-term consequences and aspirations.

3. **Scenario Visualization:** Vividly imagine what would happen with each of the available alternatives. Imagine both the rational consequences of the courses of action but also the emotional reactions to the scenarios you're envisioning. This method's analysis is matched with emotional intuition.

4. **The "Wise Mind" Approach:** This Dialectical Behavior Therapy term refers to the middle ground between one's "emotional mind" and "reasonable mind." Choices in this "wise mind" zone incorporate both emotional wisdom and reason.

5. **Stakeholder Empathy Mapping:** If other people could be impacted or affected by your decision, create empathy maps for those people. It will help you in thinking at both ends: the rational outcomes of your decision and the emotional ends as well.

6. **The "Regret Minimization" Framework:** Popularized by Jeff Bezos, this consists of projecting yourself to old age and considering which decision you will least regret. This touches on both emotional foresight and logical extrapolation.

7. **Emotional-Logical Journaling:** Keep a decision journal that includes your emotional state and the logic behind your decisions. This may be helpful in pointing out patterns over time and helping you combine your emotions and logic better in making decisions.

Master these techniques, and you will make decisions that are not only rational but emotionally satisfying as well. And that can give you the confidence to lead a better life.

❖ Practicing self-reflection to understand the motivations behind emotional reactions

Self-reflection is a very powerful tool in bringing into the surface the normally hidden drivers of emotions, which influence our thoughts and actions. This capability will help us better understand our emotional nature and how it affects our reasoning. Listed here are some practices that could raise one's self-reflection:

1. **The "Five Whys" Technique:** Whenever one has a strong emotion, try asking "Why?" five times. This can be done to discover any deeper motivations and beliefs under mere emotional reactions.

2. **Emotional Tracking:** Keep an emotion log with regard to where they were experienced and also the level of intensity of the same. In the end, after some time, it could really prove helpful in showing the patterns and triggers of your emotional responses.

3. **Meditation with Body Scan:** Practice the body scan meditation regularly to increase your sensitivity to the physical feelings that accompany different emotions. This type of physical awareness can sometimes serve as a sort of early warning system against emotional overreactions.

4. **Values Clarification Exercise:** Periodically undertake an exercise in reviewing and updating your core values. Knowledge of your core beliefs can be useful in putting into perspective why certain situations trigger high Emotional Reactivity in you.

5. **Cognitive Restructuring Practice:** Test your automatic thoughts against the available evidence for and against. This method in CBT helps to distinguish between thought which is emotionally driven and what actually is.

6. **Emotional Root Cause Analysis:** Whenever a strong emotional reaction is thrown your way, find its source. Most of the time, the current emotional response has a root in the past experience.

7. **Mindfulness of the Transition of Emotion:** Notice times of emotional state change. Transition points can really bring enlightenment to emotional triggers and patterns.

The more consistent one is with these self-reflection practices, the better one will understand their emotional motivations and allow the feelings and logic to be integrated intentionally into our decision processes.

- ❖ **Embracing the complexity of human emotions and the value they bring to making decisions.**

As we conclude our investigation into the emotional and the rational, let it not escape our memory to salute the complexity of human emotions and the pricelessness of their value in decision-making:

1. **Emotional Intuition:** Emotions at times do the job of processing information faster than a conscious mind can, providing quick insights, often critical in situations of urgency.

2. **Value Aligned:** Emotions are inner guides to making decisions that align with our central values and long-term well-being.

3. **Motivational Force:** Emotions energize and motivate the will to translate logic into action.

4. **Social Navigation:** Emotional intelligence helps us sail across complex situations, where logic can overlook subtle social cues.

5. **Catalyst of Creativity:** Emotions may trigger the creativity that leads to novel problem-solving insights which pure logic might not uncover.

6. **Moral Reasoning:** Many of the ethical decisions are dependent upon emotional responses, for example, empathy and a sense of fairness.

7. **Forming Memories:** Emotions have a significant role in the formation and recall of memory and therefore influence what experiences we learn and carry forward.

8. **Building Resilience:** Processing and learning from a wide range of emotions enhance psychological resilience and adaptability.

9. **Holistic Well-being:** The ability to recognize and acknowledge our feelings supports mental health and life satisfaction.

By embracing the fullness of our emotions and their value, we can move beyond such a false dichotomy of emotion vs. logic. Instead, we can cultivate a decision-making approach that speaks to the power of both, leading us toward choices that are not only on a rational level but also deeply fulfilling.

In closing, our journey through the landscape of emotions and logic reveals a rich tapestry of human cognition. We have witnessed the pitfalls of cognitive biases and emotional distortions, found strategies for integrating our emotions with logic and deepened our appreciation for our emotional complexity.

Here's an interesting thought: What if our emotions were not merely complementary to logic but a form of logic in and of themselves an ancient, intuitive calculus, polished by millions of years of evolution? Perhaps in the synthesis of emotion and reason, we do not have to master opposites at all. One unlocks a higher form of intelligence that goes beyond the limits of pure reason and includes the deep wisdom of our emotional selves.

May we bring to each of these choices the humility needed to recognize our biases, the courage to face our emotions and the wisdom to synthesize them into a holistic understanding. Then only shall we have a chance not only at better decisions but at deeper meanings about ourselves and the intricate beauty that is the human mind acts of life.

Made in the USA
Columbia, SC
21 August 2024

2320dd32-f7ce-480f-82e7-0a07b4f16d06R01